Preface

INDYCIA & the global Monetary System is a short book on the background of how and why US Dollar attained a pole position in the global monetary system and why an unreformed monetary system is poised to devolve.

The purpose of this book was to design for ourselves and share with inventors globally, the design characteristics of a new product that could bring about a positive change in the monetary system without causing any major upheavals.

This book has been used as an instruction manual by the authors in order to develop a product intended to change how investments and currency exchanges happen globally. The design characteristics are shared herein to evoke interest amongst experts to adopt and/or improve the Indycia instrument in an open manner.

This Book is dedicated to

Kautilya

(also called Chanakya),

one of the earliest economists in recorded Indian history, who was born in 371 BC in Taxila (undivided India).

Contents

4

Deepak Loomba is a technopreneur-founder of AICorps EPL. He has authored multiple books, published more than 50 papers, patents and other IPR. His previous works have been well received by academicians and industrialists alike with his book 'Transformers' getting half-page review in Mint.

Côme Carpentier De Gourdon is a French citizen, geo-strategic analyst an author of various books. He has written more than two hundred articles, essays and papers published in diverse journals and newspapers on geopolitical, strategic, cultural and social issues. His latest titles are From India to Infinity; Memories of a Hundred and One Moons - An Indian Odyssey and A Shining City on a Hill - Novus Ordo Seculorum.

INDYCIA is an economic essay by Deepak Loomba to which Carpentier has made various contributions and additions.

This text is an introduction to a product that the authors are intending to launch soon. This book describes the background & characteristics of a new, out-of-the-box financial instrument adapted to new techno-economic global realities. The objective of this book is to raise an open challenge for interested parties to create competitive products such as Indycia, for the best to emerge and win.

Readers are requested to generously provide their views, critiques & ideas on the link below. A QR code of the link is provided for your convenience.

INDYCIA

& the global monetary system

https://www.facebook.com/Indycia-108540784097382

INDYCIA

& the global Monetary System

SCAN QR BELOW OR GO TO THE LINK PROVIDED TO POST YOUR OPINIONS,

REVIEWS AND CRITIQUE

https://www.facebook.com/Indycia-108540784097382

To connect with us on email Scan QR below or mail@ connect@indycia.com

Indycia

& The Global Monetary System

§1. Idea to Action

Ideas that metamorphose into actions most often arise through one of the following three routes –

1.1. the entity (person) stating the problem is different from the one providing a solution;

1.2. most common - born out of statement of a problem which is discovered and followed by invention of a solution; both done by one and same person (or entity);

1.3. the solution is discovered by serendipity, while the problem is found/created subsequently – this is the rarest form of invention, where an idea is born before the problem is known. This is new knowledge. If knowledge was a bobbin of thread, then the first two kinds of inventions or discoveries represent new twirls of thread on a pre-existing bobbin, while the third one is all together a new bobbin.

Analogies:

In my book 'Transformers' (ISBN: 978-1514861240), I termed the former two as Limbic Markets (or Limbic Solutions) such that demand is the driving force that is used to invigorate supply. It means demand is the cause for suppliers to manufacture and supply goods. Such markets/solutions are limited by the imagination of the consumers/buyers/customers and are thus devoid of innovation.

The third option mentioned above is termed 'Cerebral Markets' by me in 'Transformers'. These are created by the supply side taking an initiative to create a completely novel innovative product without existing customer / consumer demand. Demand is enkindled for the new product/service after it is introduced to the market by the supplier / innovator. As the product introduction initiative is coming from the supplier, the product is not limited by the needs of the consumer and shifts orbit into the imagination of an Innovative Supplier.

It is apparent that 'Cerebral Markets' are advanced markets that hinge on creativity and innovation, have lower competition but are highly time-sensitive.

'Limbic Markets' on the other hand are largely commodity markets, less time sensitive and beholden to major competition as there is little technology or IPR that needs to be developed. At the level of an individual product (in microcosm) 'Cerebral Market' Products/Services are uncertain in their adoption and success, while Limbic

Market Products/Services face eminent risks. Therefore, whereas the former propel a quantum leap in growth, the latter are evolutionary – bit by bit. The former are difficult to copy and repeat, and are usually followed by very few nations.

A similar analogy exists in Economic Growth Models. There is a demand/consumption led growth model whose foundations are laid on economic growth happening from the rise in demand. Limbic Markets are subject to consumers' needs and hence are not agile in terms of innovations and entrepreneurship. Demand is always limited to public knowledge and to existing consumption patterns of customers for goods and services, making this economic growth model 'Limbic' in nature. Investment-led growth model on the contrary pre-supposes the presence of capable innovators & entrepreneurs with availability of risk-capital and inexpensive debt capital. Thereby, it is left to the supplier's imagination to pre-empt the needs of the consumers and create new products and services. This model also coerces the Supplier market to cast its wings wide for exports. To counter uncertainty in one market, smart investors/suppliers of 'Cerebral Markets' create foothold in multiple nations / markets. This ensures that in case a product or service fails to gain acceptance in one country, it can succeed in another. The Cerebral Growth Model therefore, coerces product and service suppliers to draw ambitious export plans and keep access to available foreign markets.

It also can be deduced that Cerebral Markets have higher business churn-rates than Limbic. Businesses are created fast and also may shut down fast. This results from average higher failure rate of businesses in Cerebral Markets.

It merits mention that both Limbic and Cerebral Economic Agents coexist within one and the same economic ecosystem. What makes a market limbic or cerebral is the proportion of limbic and cerebral economic agents. Most middle income nations have both types of economic agents.

There is one more disparity between the Limbic & Cerebral – the latter is never an intended result of research, if at all any research goes into it. And this is the reason why it is challenging to bring such ideas to life – they happen unintendedly.

Indycia can be classified as a cerebral product, though there is an existing perceptual demand (created by temporary geopolitical or intra-national circumstances – almost like a force majeure).

§2. Discoveries

A few years ago I received an invitation to be part of a committee to consider the prospect of trade between India and Russia in local currencies, I was pretty amazed and might I say scared by what came out of these meetings. I had seen the result of such arrangements between India and the Soviet Union. USSR supplied arms and other exports to India against Indian Rupees, such that all such Rupees were paid in Vnesheconombank's escrow account in the Reserve Bank of India. These Rupees could be spent by Russia only for purchase of goods from India through a letter of credit. It was a great deal for India, as it could buy critical defence equipment in a very favourable barter arrangement. The Indian Rupee represented nothing but a unit for the purpose of barter. We got to buy planes and other advanced equipment for tea, coffee & sweaters.

But when the Soviet Union disintegrated and fell into economic trouble, in early 90s, the Indian Rupees held by Russia as the successor state to the USSR, were of little value. Once Russia opened to trade with the west, Indian products were no more aspirational and the market for them crashed. Freed markets in Russia no more wanted to buy Indian Products. Therefore, the Indian Rupees held by Russia were sold at a discount. In the most tumultuous years of the late 80s and early nineties an Indian Rupee could be purchased for Rs 0.20 in US Dollars.

The rate of US$ in India was in the range of `25 for a US$ in early nineties, while the Russian owners of Indian Rupees (which could be encashed only if goods were shipped from India to Russia and a payment effected through a letter of credit), would part with `25 letter of credit for 0.20US$. These were the best exchange rates I had known then. I would not be surprised if there were others which were even better because in Russia these Rupees were held by large corporates who were suddenly freed to manage their affairs without any oversight. Malpractices, therefore were common.

This led to three major outcomes – (i) a major spurt in round-tripping, (ii) Hawala[1] Operations, (iii) dumping of unneeded, poor quality goods of Indian origin which destroyed the market for Indian goods in Russia. The image of Indian goods is still recovering from this negative memory, close to three decades later.

The mathematics of the aforementioned phenomena was simple. Entrepreneurs gave `28 instead of `25 to a hawala operator, got 1 US$ in Dubai or London, transferred it to their associate (subsidiary) in Russia, use it to buy a `125 worth of letter of credit to export goods to India. Hence, the money after all facilitation payments, was at least tripled through letter of credit in India. The goods brought in were of no consequence. Smart traders realized that they could

---

[1] Conversion of unaccounted currency at a rate different from official conversion rate, such that no bank transfer is involved. Hence, Indian Rupees were bought by illegal financial operators, against which US$ were made available in a foreign account (or even in cash) in US$, UK Pounds or Dinars (Hard currencies). The practise is common till date in all those countries which do not allow current account convertibility of their currency.

export grossly over-invoiced, exceptionally cheap goods. That is how poor quality bedsheets, brooms, sweaters and other ultra-cheap goods were shipped from India to Russia, the payment effected to oneself, amounting to three rupees output for every one invested. Goods in Russia, in some cases, were not even custom cleared. There were hundreds of containers from India that were forsaken at the St. Petersburg port and never claimed by fictitious importers, because claiming them would lead to payment of duty and consequent sale. The savvier operators were not interested in either of them. Since the quantities of these goods were huge, customs would ultimately auction them. These third rate goods which no one bought even in India, ended up in the Russian market. Exporting was reduced to a solely financial operation.

With passage of time, as more and more Indians came to know of this money making machine, the discount rate kept on falling and subsequently stabilized at 5-7% all throughout late nineties and early 2000s. The discount accounted for the inconvenience of Letter of Credit payment and the mandatory export of goods to realize the value.

I felt this battered not only the image of Indian goods, but also of Indian currency in Russia.

The irony was that the Government / bureaucrats / diplomats were happy and considered this as an achievement for a good and a bad reason. The good one was that India paid up every penny it owed to the USSR, making it a good debtor. The bad one was that they did not realize how this damaged

India's commercial image in Russia in the long term. Trade between India and Russia even today stands at a paltry 10billion US$, which is unimpressive when one compares the trade of Russia with Europe, China and many other states, even under mutual sanctions applied by EU and US since forceful takeover of Crimea by Russia from Ukraine and the following bitter war still fought in Ukraine. I constantly hear Ministers and Bureaucrats wondering why Indo-Russian trade is not picking up. The answer that most of them do not want to hear is – this is the cost we are paying for unnatural dividends some Indian and Russian enterprises earned from Russian distress during country's most difficult years. They were burdened with Indian Rupees, which no one in Russia was interested in. Was this grey business rampant? My answer would be, 'no'. This was the pre-internet era and information did not spread as fast. Yet, there were organizations in India which took home obscene amounts of money through such schemes.

"Was India planning another such enterprise?" I thought to myself with anguish. There was no dearth of business people who proposed to resurrect the model of past. And why not – for a chosen few it works all too well, but for the nation it bodes ill; especially for future export opportunities.

The meeting I attended was held at Confederation of Indian Industry at the Lodi Estate Head Office, with members from Industry, the Department of Financial services, the Ministry of External Affairs, the State Bank of India, the Reserve Bank of India and a few other agencies.

It was apparent that invoicing exported goods to Russia in Indian Rupees or Russian Roubles is not prohibited and is being done by a few companies. Dr. Reddy's Lab was said to invoice exported pharmaceutical products in Russian Roubles (I did not confirm it from the management at the time of writing this book). So per se, there were no obstacles to invoicing goods in Indian or Russian currency. For a company which is accruing a major chunk of its revenue from Indian and Russian markets and investing both Rubles in Russia and Rupees in India, it isn't much of an issue but the moment one starts calculating notional losses or profits had the same goods been exported in US$, the scenario changes dramatically because of the changing exchange rates of the Ruble to US$ vis-à-vis Rupee to US$. The problem gathers steam once project exports are to be executed, payments for which are received over 3-5 years.

The moment one wants to calculate his or her Rupees in Rubles or vice-versa the problem evolves - How to do it? The usual way is to arrive at a Ruble to Rupee conversion rate by dividing the Ruble to US$ rate with Rupee to US$ one and get Rubles for Rupees. Logically this seems to be fine. But the psychological challenge which many face with this is – why should the exchange rate of Ruble to Rupee depend on an intermediary – the US$? Why can't the Rupee-Ruble exchange rate be based on trade & investment amongst India and Russia respectively.

Why should there be a dependence on US Dollar to determine the exchange rate of Indian Rupees and Russian Rubles.

The meeting ended with no major breakthrough, but recommendations were made by CII as a consequence of the meeting, for the Government to consider and act accordingly.

With an inclination to derive and operate from first principles and thanks to my mathematical-physics background, coupled with sound logic, I knew well that there are no direct exchange rates amongst currencies. Each currency is linked for its conversion rate to the US Dollar and their mutual conversion rates are derived from their respective exchange rates vis-à-vis the US Dollar. The latter is the international 'Major' & Base Currency.

The other fact that comes out is that US Dollar's status as a base currency has little to do with it's standing as the world's premier reserve currency. The status of US Dollar as a base currency came from the Bretton Woods and the subsequent Nixon Shock of August 1971 when the gold underwriting of US Dollar as set by the Bretton Woods Agreement was terminated and a system of freely floating fiat was forced on the world.

The use of US Dollar as a reserve currency happened owing to the willingness of the US to run a huge current account deficit while concurrently ensuring that the largest and most critical commodity of 20th century – Oil was priced and sold strictly in US Dollars leading to rise of Petro-Dollars.

Imagine that every time a human being transports himself or any goods on the face of earth, the expense accruing thereby is strictly calculated and paid in US Dollars, not in local currency. While a user buying fuel at a gas station may believe he is paying in Dinars or Rupiahs or Swedish Kronas, in reality, the company supplying fuel to him pays in US Dollars for the fuel it bought.

Even those countries, which are oil-producing and might arbitrarily value the commodity in their local currencies, still pay in US Dollars. Because the lower costs (for locally produced fuels) are nothing but a subsidy given by the Governments to their people, as the Government could have always sold this commodity at market prices. Since, 1950s oil began to replace coal as the main energy source.

If you have been able to imagine that everyone in your country has been paying strictly in US Dollars for travelling from home to office (or any place for that matter) daily for last 5+ decades, you can understand the amount of US Dollars this has created in the world. It is pertinent to mention that Petro-Dollars stand for only one of thousands of categories of transactions that are executed in US Dollars.

§3. Multi-currency exchange rates in existing frameworks

All financial transactions are fundamentally transactions of exchange. The 'price' of any physical or financial asset is reached from the exchange value that a buyer is ready to buy at and a seller is ready to sell at.

The value of any currency, if it is not exchanged (or exchanged only in meagre amounts) with any other can be arbitrarily valued as per the desire of the Sovereign.

A change of value of the currency internally, without any change externally - relative to another nation's currency, is nothing but a change in denomination. A good example that I lived through is that of Russia, which twice changed the denomination of its currency. All nations which have undergone hyperinflation undergo rapid uncontrolled devaluation of their currency. At a very fast pace (sometimes a few times a day) the value of currency keeps on sliding leading to very large exchange values (sometimes in hundreds of thousands of units of one currency vis-à-vis another). Often for ease of calculations, countries change the denomination of their currency. They issue new notes, such that the public can go to any bank and change their old bills; say thousand Rubles (as was in Russia in late 90s) for a 1 New Russian Ruble, which invariably differs in design to distinguish from the old. In such cases the loaf of bread that earlier cost 5000 Rubles will now be priced at 5 New Rubles. Such a change of denomination does not impact the economy. It is mere change of scale of measure, as when we refer to a 1 metre length as 3.28 feet.

Exchange Rate means little, without trends

In fact, the value of any currency vis-à-vis another one at a point of time indicates nothing much of the state or history of economic progress of either of the compared currencies. There were a few thousand Italian Liras (the Italian Currency before adoption of the Euro) in one US Dollar. But that did not make the Italian economy better or worse, stable or unstable. The only thing this large number equivalence revealed is that Italy in its history had some period of extreme hyper-inflation leading to devaluation and nothing more. It does not state the current condition of economy, which can be assessed only by observing the trends of exchange rates in recent periods.

The rate for any commodity is the weighted balance-point of demand & supply, subject to the said rate not having caused an unreasonably[2] negative value to the manufacturer/creator of the commodity across a reasonable period of time. Irrespective of whether the commodity is physical, intangible or financial. An easy spatial cognition of rate discovery that I personally use to understand demand and supply is the need to move the fulcrum (rate) to keep a

---

[2]One can reasonably assume that if the rate of a commodity is constantly less than its cost of production, then such production (in market economies) can only be sustained for a duration that erodes all the positive value (profit) created by the product for the enterprise. Thereafter, the enterprise will have no option but to stop production. Seizure of production reduces the volume available in the market, thereby improving the rate.

demand-supply seesaw, stably in equilibrium, such that rate is defined as the distance between the fulcrum and the weight of supply. Equal weights on demand and supply will cause the fulcrum to be in the centre. As the weight on the demand side increases, the fulcrum will have to be shifted towards the demand side increasing the rate (distance between fulcrum and supply weights). Increase of supply side weights will require the fulcrum to be moved towards the supply side reducing the rate (distance between the supply side weights and the fulcrum). The mechanism is depicted below in the image.

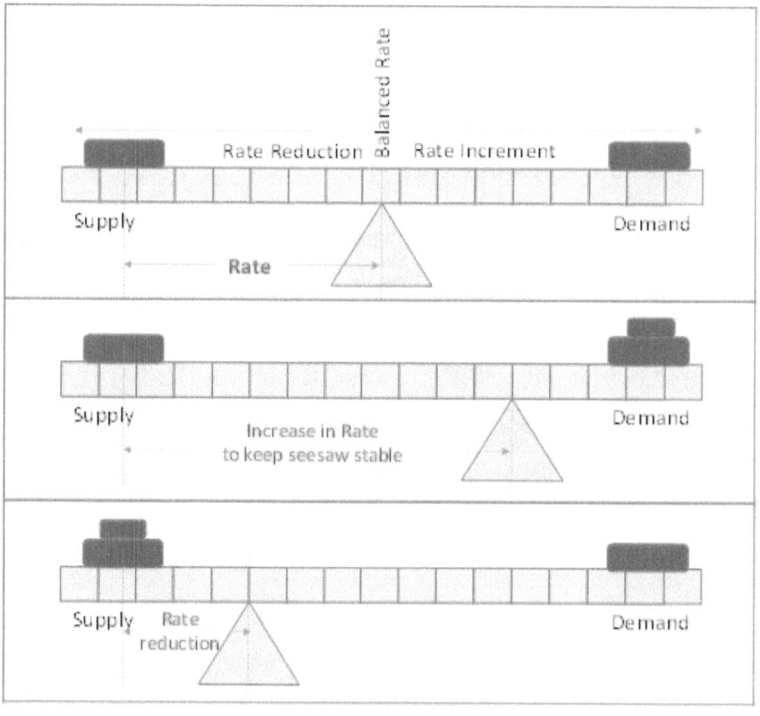

Image 01

So let's take an example of rate of US Dollars and Indian Rupees. Export and import of **Assets**[3] between India and United States should have determined the exchange rate between the two but it doesn't because as in the US there is a demand for Indian Rupees to pay for **Assets** imported from India as there is a demand from China too to pay for similar **Asset** imports from India. Therefore, the aggregate demand from all nations determines the demand for Indian Rupees globally. Conversely, there is a demand for US Dollars to import **Assets** from US. Other nations too have similar demands for US Dollars, thereby creating an aggregate demand for US Dollars globally. This creates a many-to-many relationship among all currencies. Any change in the demand for one ripples into change in demand of all others. But each is related to all others including the first one that was initially changed, resulting in a circular relationship (regressive, but indeterminate).

For readers' understanding - "Have you come across circular relationship in spreadsheets (say Excel)?"

It happen when in a formula written in cell 'A' one refers to a cell 'B' which in turn carries a reference to cell 'A'. So, to circumvent this problem, one creates a macro, in which one copies and special pastes (as value) the value arrived in Cell 'B' to the right place in Cell 'A' (which had a reference to cell 'B'). Every time one special pastes this value in Cell 'A'

---

[3]Includes physical (goods), intangibles (services) and financial (capital investments, remittances and strategic + speculative currency sale-purchase) assets.

the linked value in Cell B changes. One again copies and special pastes the new value arrived in Cell 'B' to the right place in cell 'A'. This keeps on going on in a loop until and unless the change in the value in cell 'B' is marginal.

In real life, demand / transactions of currency exchange are unceasingly large, and hence the solution is not even sensibly heuristic. Hence, any solution for determining the exchange rates between currencies at any point of time in present or future, arrived from their aggregate demand at the said point (in present or future periods) has at best - a cumbersome heuristic & academic solution. It is important to remember that heuristic solutions are not ideal in finance, because of the huge amount of monies involved. A trillion USD transaction will have a huge impact even if a heuristic solution is in the 9th decimal! It is important to remember…

"Capital demands certainty".

§4. Models of Transnational Economic Relations

As was depicted in Image 01 the see-saw of demand and supply of a nation's currency in relation to other currencies is derived from the imports and exports of **Assets** [physical, intangible & financial (including remittances, investments & strategic + speculative currency sale-purchase)] and is always balanced (held in the air) by definition. The fulcrum is the exchange rate that keeps on moving with changes in the weights of imports and exports. If exports keep on increasing vis-à-vis imports of **Assets** the demand of national currency increases forcing the movement of the fulcrum (Exchange Rate) towards appreciation of the currency value. Increase in weightage of imports leads to devaluation of a nation's currency. It is important to note that speculative currency sale-purchases can impact the weightage of import and export of **assets** and hence the demand or supply of a currency. 'Speculative currency sale-purchase' is an important mechanism as it owes the reason of its existence to future anticipations (is predictive in nature). It financially spreads the future jolts & spikes over time, smoothening them (future spikes) by commencing its rise early, in the present time, in form of 'anticipation'. The speculativeness of currency sale-purchase is dependent on the quality, firmness and certainty of information of future that an economic agent has. The Reserve Bank of India (or say US Federal Reserve) has very high quality of information through all Banks that it constantly supervises. Therefore, it can predict foreseeable future monetary flows with a high degree of certainty. Therefore, any or all interventions of such State Economic

Agents like - RBI or USFR are not termed speculations. Commercial organizations lack this information and, to take advantage of future speculate on the future demand-supply of a currency.

4.1. Would the world be an ideal market

Let us assume a world where all currencies are accepted and freely traded. Let us consider a nation 'A' which, within a set duration, say of an year, would possess a whole array of currencies of those nations to which it would have sold more than bought. Concurrently, every nation, to which sales of A are less than purchase would have got A's currency in return.

Let us make another assumption that there is one electronic marketplace to sell and purchase all currencies. An electronic marketplace is reliable as it is algorithmic, rational & devoid of human emotion.

The concern of Nation 'A' would be on account of the currencies of other nations that it possesses because A's currency in other nations, anyway is not in control of A, once the currency is transferred.

4.2. Rational Action of an average Nation 'A'

Thematically, what does the currency of nation 'A' held by nation 'B' mean?

It means that either 'A' did not sell 'B' enough to balance that which it bought, or that 'B' purchases goods from 'A' so often that it wants to keep some currency of 'A' in reserve. All the currency of 'A' with 'B' is a promise of 'A' to 'B' to provide a value in future for the currency held at a future rate of exchange. Making and keeping promises is the foundation of trust and thus credibility.

Let's look at the trade seesaw of Nation 'A'. An ideal situation implies its trade to be balanced. Now let us assume that currency of 'A' is desired by other nations to be kept by them in reserve. We understand that for a currency to become a reserve currency, there have to be higher amounts of purchase of strategic + speculative assets than those that justify goods & services exported to 'A'. This apparently requires 'A' to print additional quantities of its currency, which 'A' is sure will be bought by other nations as strategic + speculative reserves. The strategic + speculative purchase is made keeping in mind the future demand in other nations of the currency of 'A' but would this extra currency not be absorbed by the nations wanting to admit it to their reserves? Availability of this additional unwanted, unbalanced amount of A's currency would have moved the fulcrum towards (higher supply) lesser exchange rate value of A's currency to keep the system stable. However, because the additional printed currency of A was lapped up by others for their strategic + speculative reserves, the movement of the fulcrum is deferred indefinitely, for future period of time.

How could reserves of A's currency be built by others?

a) Through grants from 'A' (the Marshall Plan is a good example).

b) Higher **Asset**[4] exports to 'A' than imports (like Japan, China, India, which have built their reserves of US Dollars)

c) Through a currency swap – such that A & one more nation decide to hold each other's currency in reserves.

In case of strategic & speculative reserves as well as currency swaps, there is no supply of the printed currency to the markets, therefore no immediate inflation occurs.

In case of currency swaps, the future inflation potential is limited only to the extent of rate change through the period of swap.

The economic seesaw mechanism also demonstrates how oversupply of either goods or currency causes a fall in its rate. To keep the seesaw in the air, one is coerced to move the rate fulcrum towards the added supply, thereby reducing the rate.

In an ideal world, guided by rational thought, a sensible fundamental premise for a socially stable and prospering nation should be –get value in exchange for currency rather than a promise (which currency currently is). Purchase of currency of another nation is buying into its sovereign risks. Why would a stable society buy into the sovereign risks of another national society, about which they have little or no understanding? Kindly pay attention to the fact that my

---

[4]Including physical (goods), intangible (services) & financial (incl. remittances, investments, strategic + speculative reserves.

assertion is about 'preferring' value to promise (currency) rather than prohibiting. Therefore, ideally a socially stable nation should have reserves just large enough to tide over any temporary force majeure for a few months (say 1-2 quarters). Anything beyond that is trying to exchange one's own insecurity for the uncertainty & risk of another nation (represented by the currencies of these nations in one's reserves). It is akin to building a dam to save a village from mild, but regular flooding. The dam works well, till a black swan happens. If the dam breaks it is a calamity of great magnitude. A dam is a blessing but also a weapon of mass destruction and is dependent on the use made of the stored up water.

Multi-currency discovery of an exchange rate seems achievable in case the aforementioned premise (get value in exchange for currency rather than a promise) is taken into consideration.

Would economies agree to operate on a rational basis? Let us assume that Nation 'A' has following currencies in its hand at the end of the year (or for that matter, at any point of time):

(1) Currency of Nation 'B' 200 units
(2) Currency of Nation 'C' 152 units
(3) Currency of Nation 'D' 111 units
(4) Currency of Nation 'E' 11 units

Following are the nations, which have Nation A's currencies at the end of year:

(5) Nation 'F' has 500 units of A's currency

(6) Nation 'G' has 245 units of A's currency

(7) Nation 'H' has 45 units of A's currency

A is among the categories of nations that have deficit with some and proficit (latin for surplus) with some and most normal nations fall in this category. There are a few who have deficit against all (or most) or proficit against all (most). We will talk about them separately.

Amongst those with deficit against some nations and proficit against others, two approaches are available to them, explained thereafter. First category of nations is forward-looking, unmindful of history and generally confident in the future. Because they are well placed currently and it is very natural to project a favourable present (includes recent past) into a better future. Such nations are riskophilic[5] else they will not exhibit the aforementioned characteristics.

The other category of nations is that of history-buffs. They are always mindful of lessons history taught and invariably projecting their future not from their present (including the recent past) but from centuries of history (Braudel's 'très longue durée'). This category is extraordinarily mindful of risks and often exhibits riskophobia[6].

The riskophobics view concepts and rules of existence (including trust, creditworthiness etc.) as rigid and non-negotiable.

---

[5]Daring as a society. Collective, social approval to affinity to risking.
[6]Periculophobia

The former category, the riskophilics, view the world as changing and malleable, are highly cognizant of impermanence of situations and are willing to negotiate everything, which the riskophobics consider non-negotiable.

It is important to note that neither of them are right or wrong. In certain circumstances the former are in an advantageous position, while in others, the latter are better placed. Surely the riskophilic grow fast, go through depressions, are more focused on the deliverables in the near future, are more accustomed to mission-mode[7] execution of projects with a maximum duration of 3-5 years, and usually lack very long term (say10-20year) vision-mode[8] planning. The riskophobic grow slowly but steadily and have a tendency not to fail completely. Such societies are successful only in vision-mode, and almost always fail or underperform in mission-mode, because their constitution and cultural behaviour is guided not by the short or medium-term objectives but by higher values, perspectives and moral or ideological beliefs..

It is pertinent to mention that nations and societies periodically undergo social changes (upheavals, sometimes) leading to change in collective social attitude from riskophilic to riskophobic or vice-versa.

It merits mention that Indian society, collectively, in its recent (and current) historical period is constitutionally

---

[7]With clarity of objectives that are desired to be achieved.
[8]Understanding of larger goals, while objectives are malleable & alterable.

riskophobic. Culturally, we have always championed the 'middle path' – 'Santulan' (balance in Hindi) as a virtue.

In the next paragraphs we will discuss the trends and tendencies of nations in the first and second category.

4.3. What happens if Nation 'A' is riskophilic

Would Nation 'A' be riskophilic, deductive logic drives one to conclude that it will desire to algorithmically maximize its advantage in the marketplace, by preferring value (usable goods and services) to currency (promise) on receipts and currency over value on payments because that is how others get invested into A's future and would therefore be receptive to the concerns and issues of 'A' . 'A' in such circumstance would be inclined to prefer goods for itself and promises to others (the US chose this path). Therefore, Nation 'A' in such circumstances would desire to execute one of the below-mentioned two with the extra currency it has in hand from B, C, D and E, while it has no control over its currency held by F, G and H.

Another fork is found here with three possibilities. Options for Nation 'A' in such circumstances would be to

4.3.1. Sell the currencies of B, C, D, and E in the market to replace buy back its own currency from F, G, and H, with the currencies of B, C, D and E. It is F, G and H's products that 'A' is importing more than it is exporting to them and therefore, it has to give promises in exchange for the value of extra import (that which is not balanced by exports to them) in the form of the currency of A which is then held by F, G & H. By selling currencies of B, C, D, and E, A does reduce his debt to F, G and H, but will end up diverting business to B, C, D, and E, as F, G & H possessing currencies of B, C, D and E will be inclined to make purchases from them. This is still a balanced approach, which tends to reduce one's deficit to others by using the currencies with whom Nation 'A' has a proficit.

4.3.2. Sell the currencies of B, C, D, and E in the market to buy goods from whosoever is ready to sell, rather than exchange them for some other currency, including A's own with F, G & H. This ensures that they do not hold currency, but consume goods (US chose this path). This leads to holding the deficit as it was, and enhance consumption, as more goods are made available to consume and concurrently, F, G & H are kept invested in the future of 'A' through the promises of 'A' they hold. This creates a self-propagating mechanism, where A wants to sell more and more to B, C, D & E, constantly increasing the proficit with them on one hand and selling their currency in the market to buy more goods and enhance consumption in Nation A. While A also keeps on enhancing purchase from F, G & H and consequently its dues towards them. This state is enjoyable and easy to be in. People of 'A' are happy because they are provided easy credits to consume more and more. Consumption tickles the pleasure centres of the brain and is addictive. Rising consumption expands the hunger and market for more goods, giving other nations (F, G, H) an opportunity to sell more and more in A's market.

4.3.3. The third option is not mutually exclusive from the second, which means both can be executed simultaneously. Under the current option, Nation 'A' uses the currencies of B, C, D and E to buy fixed assets in the respective nations to produce goods to export back to themselves. In this way they reduce their holdings of currencies of B, C, D and E by ultimately converting them into goods that are shipped to 'A'. In the process they sell domestically within the nations of B, C, D, and E, earning profits in local currencies, which are then converted into A's currency, Thus increasing the demand of A's currency internally within B, C, D & E and thus reducing the holdings of B, C, D and E's currency with 'A'.

F, G, and H are anyways invested into A's future as they hold A's promises against which they have drawn a proficit. Generally, F, G & H would be allowed to invest in 'A' so that investment flows into 'A', increasing the employed assets in 'A' and further expanding A's economy and consumption.

4.4. What happens if Nation 'A' is riskophobic

Would Nation 'A' be riskophobic, it would always desire to algorithmically reduce its risks in the marketplace, by preferring value (usable goods and services) to currency (promise) on payments and currency over value on receipts because that is how they can keep their future obligations and risks at a minimum. They are very careful about their credibility and trust and are generally inclined to grow slowly, but steadily.

Would 'A' be such a nation, it would then keep the currencies of B, C, D & E for future purchases; concurrently, it would strive to reduce its deficit with F, G & H, because of them suddenly demanding (dumping) A's currency to be replaced with goods or other currencies. They do not invest in B, C, D & E with the reason – "what if they ('A') suddenly need more currencies of B, C, D & E"? Simultaneously, they do not let F, G & H invest back into them, as that would let them own fixed assets in nation 'A' and eventually become the owners of the Nation 'A'.

Because of their cultural attitude to life and economics, they are always inclined to correct their situation, not change it. This distinction is very important. Those intending to correct, think only of evolutionary means to alter a trend and do mid-course corrections to avoid losses and consolidate gains in every two steps if their decisions are beneficial. Those wanting to change look at out-of-the-box solutions and are inclined to implement them bearing the risk of failure, if required. Altering can never lead to failure, it can lead to slight improvement or slight deterioration but not utter failure.

An important outcome from the aforementioned is that the most deadly combination that goes unchallenged is the one where partners nations belonging to opposite camps complement each other. The riskophobic do exactly that which resonates complementarily with the natural frequency of the riskophilic and vice-versa. This creates long spells of collaborative growth. It provides ideal returns, but is also an exceptionally high risk model, because it generally lacks competition in riskophilia. The riskophilic grows so big so fast that one riskophilic is equal to many riskophobics in terms of economic size. Equilibrium can exist at different energy levels of a system. A span bridge is stable with two cars or 300 trucks. But the tension in the system with 300 trucks is so high that if the steel cables snap, they will destroy everything that comes on their way.

4.5. Nations with perennial proficits with most others
Such nations that sell their products all over the world and have proficits with most (China being a glaring example) end up with large number of promises from all nations globally against loss of their natural resources (natural resources are detailed further ahead). Since this category is very small concerning either very large or very small nations; in the comity they often end up in one-against-many relationships. These are largely exporting nations (China again comes to mind), collecting a constant inflow of currency. To keep up the perennial nature of their proficit, they have to keep the exchange rate of their own currency stable. To make this happen, large exporting nations like China and South Korea, keep their currency exchange rate

pegged to US Dollar at a pre-determined rate, such that their Central Banks keep on buying the forex for strategic reserves. In reality, constant proficit generally raises the rate of their currency vis-à-vis others'. Hence, they run a risk of everyone ganging up against them to find ways to annul their promises towards one. Such nations have little option, but to invest in fixed assets of the nations they have proficits with. Because if they release the currencies perennially into marketplace, it will lead to constant appreciation of their currency exchange rate vis-à-vis others, making them less competitive in international trade. If they do not invest the currency in reserves from their proficits, in the fixed assets of other nations, what else would they do with low yield promises of everyone in the world? That indeed is what China is trying to do through its Belt and Road Plan. US had similarly launched the Marshall Plan in the fifties to invest the proficit it was running against all European nations. Owing to the technological strides and mass production that America had made during WWII, America was the best source for all types of goods needed by Europeans. Therefore, under the Marshall plan to kick start a process, US gave large grants to Europe, which they used to make purchases of US projects and goods. Similarly, nations with perennial proficits end up owning huge number of investments in immovable assets with sovereign risks of other nations. This leads to either such nations (like China) losing investments or ending up in military conflicts to save them (US did this on various occasions and China will do it when such a need arises), every time a major investment is jeopardized by political instability. It is not an ideal position to be in.

4.6. Nations with perennial deficits with most others.

Such nations that constantly run deficits would end up providing their currencies to all nations thereby, creating a market where all economic agents are sellers. This is unsustainable As the supply of their currency keeps on endlessly increasing with less and less buyers, the rate of their currency (the fulcrum) will keep on endlessly moving towards supply side (reducing) in the Economic Seesaw equivalent, used earlier for ease of understanding.

The currency of such deficit economies keeps on endlessly depreciating and losing value vis-à-vis others. It will leave holders of their currency with no option but to use it to buy its fixed assets. To make it simple – such nations end up losing control on their resources against their own consumption, which is largely satisfied with import of goods. Pakistan seems to illustrate such a case, in India's neighbourhood.

Both 4.5. and 4.6. are outliers, while 4.3. and 4.4. might be riskophilic or riskophobic, but generally are not outliers.

4.7. Nations like humans are not always rational

Nations too, like human do not behave in set patterns. Therefore, there are innumerable deviations from the models described in 4.2, 4.3, 4.4 but they are mere deviations from fundamental models - the ones presented above. The other assumption made to create the aforementioned model is the existence of perfectly free world markets. This too will never be fully achieved. Therefore, the real model will always be a deviance from one the aforementioned.

4.8. Exchange Rates and Forex Reserves

There is another tacit assumption in the model above – that everyone has trust in everyone else's currency in the marketplace. Since this is not true, many operators in the market with holdings of various other currencies, convert these currencies into those in which they have higher trust. These higher trust currencies to which holders of other currencies desire to convert them become Reserve Currencies, while the currencies that are preferred not to be held, have a constant 'sell' pressure on them. This too would lead to situation very similar to that explained in 4.6.

This brings us to important conclusions:

4.8.1. Currencies fail on international marketplaces either because of unsustainable, perennial deficit with all trading partners or for lack of trust of the market operators in the said currency – something that is caused usually by political instability.

4.8.2. Would nations agree on the ideal free market and the postulates mentioned in the models above, it would be possible to create an automated algorithmic market of currency exchange, where rates are derived as direct-relationships amongst currencies eliminating US Dollar as a Major Base currency.

It is understood by the author that agreement on such a no-favour to any, neutral model for value and currency exchange globally or even amongst a group of nations might be difficult to forge.

§5. Bretton Woods Agreement & Dollarization of World Economy

The Bretton Woods agreement of 1944 established a new post-war global monetary system, replacing the gold standard with U.S. Dollar as the international currency. By so doing, it established America as the dominant power in the world economy. After the agreement was signed, America was the only country with the ability to print Dollars.

The agreement created the World Bank and the International Monetary Fund (IMF). These U.S.-backed organizations would monitor the new system. The former was designed to monitor exchange rates and lend reserve currencies to nations with trade deficits, the latter to provide underdeveloped nations with needed capital — although each institution's role has changed over time. Each of the 44 nations which joined the discussions contributed a membership fee, of sorts, to fund these institutions; the amount of each contribution corresponded to a country's economic size and dictated the percentage of its voting rights.

In an effort to free international trade and fund post-war reconstruction, the member states agreed to fix their exchange rates by tying their currencies to the U.S. Dollar. American politicians, meanwhile, assured the rest of the world that their currency was dependable by linking the U.S. Dollar to gold. Thirty Five US Dollar equalled one ounce of Bullion. US undertook to provide one ounce of Gold to anyone wanting to exchange a US Dollar. Nations also agreed to buy and sell U.S. Dollars to keep their currencies within 1% of the fixed rate. And thus the golden age of the U.S. Dollar began.

British economist John Maynard Keynes drafted much of the plan, terming it, "opposite of gold standard," saying the negotiated monetary system would be whatever the controlling nations wished to make of it. Keynes had even gone so far as to propose a single, global currency that wouldn't be tied to either gold or politics. The latter idea of course never materialized.

Coming on the heels of the Great Depression and at the end of World War II, the Bretton Woods system addressed global ills that dated back to the 1st World War, when governments (including the U.S.) began to control imports and exports to offset wartime blockades. This, in turn, led to the manipulation of currencies to shape foreign trade. Currency warfare and restrictive market practices helped spark the devaluation, deflation and depression that defined the economies of the 1930s.

Bretton Woods had foreseen that each US Dollar would be backed by 0.35 oz. of Bullion. But this is not how it happened. US has printed US Dollars and exported them to access global resources without having enough gold to back them.

§6. Fort Knox, Nixon Shock, Fiat Commoditization and Financialization

The Bretton Woods system collapsed in August 1971, when President Richard Nixon severed the link between the Dollar and Gold — a decision made to prevent a run on Fort Knox, which contained only a third of the gold bullion necessary to cover the amount of Dollars in foreign hands. By 1973, most major world economies had allowed their currencies to float freely against the Dollar. It was a rocky transition, characterized by plummeting stock prices, skyrocketing oil prices, bank failures and inflation.

The system of free floating fiats meant that the US Dollar had no value backing it other than that which can be exchanged by a seller anywhere in the world.

Carrying forward the Bretton Wood arrangement and the following Petrodollar arrangement, all major fiats ceased to be pegged to Gold through the US Dollar (through the 35US$ an ounce backing of the US Govt.). The relationship amongst the currencies was based on exchange value arrived at from 'buy' and 'sell' propositions in the market. Factually, thereafter, fiats have got converted into financial commodities whose prices set no differently mode than say those of Orange Concentrate or Copper on the commodity exchange. This was bound to happen.

The reason for this commoditization of fiats to happen is very well elucidated in Deepak Loomba's Unified Theory of Resources.

6.1. Unified Theory of Resources

The Unified Theory of Resources elucidated in books authored by Deepak Loomba – 'Invention of Description' (ISBN: 978-1548181130) and 'Living Volume 3 Influence and Power' (ISBN: 979-8604179987) asserts that there are 8 different types of Resources including (i) administrative, (ii) economic, (iii) legal & political, (iv) social, (v) technological, (vi) Public health and existential, (vii) emotional, (viii) Academic-Scientific-Intellectual. There is further sub-categorization of Economic Resources into four kinds: Primary (Attention & Time), Secondary (Space and Skills), Tertiary (Manpower, Machine, Services, Premises, Processes), Transactional (Money, Material, Utilities). Therefore, consumption of others' resources or change in pattern of consumption of resources is the fundamental purpose of power.

For details on the Concept of Unified Theory of Resources, you are welcome to read my book Invention of Description (ISBN 978-1514861240).

Money and materials are transactional resources - mere commodities that are used as a currency for transacting in other resources – Primary, Secondary or Tertiary. Therefore, the said commoditization was an inevitable outcome of human social and economic evolution, as societies realized that attention, time, money, goods, services, manpower, skills, etc. are all economic resources, each exchangeable for others at a variable exchange value.

§7. Petro-Dollarization of World Economy

On February 14, 1945, President Franklin D. Roosevelt formalized an alliance with Saudi Arabia's King Abd al-Aziz on the USS Quincy. US built an airfield at Dhahran in return for military and business training. It also cemented the relationship between the Dollar and oil. The Petrodollar was born. This alliance was so critical that it survived differences of opinion over the Arab-Israeli conflict. After the Nixon shock of August 1971 and by 1979, the United States and Saudi Arabia negotiated the United States-Saudi Arabian Joint Commission on Economic Cooperation. They agreed to use U.S. Dollars for oil contracts. The U.S. Dollars would be recycled back to America through contracts with the U.S. companies and purchases of US goods and services.

Since then, oil-exporting countries have become more sophisticated. They now recycle their petrodollars through sovereign wealth funds. They use these funds to invest in non-oil related businesses. The profits from these businesses make them less dependent on oil prices. Here are the world's largest petrodollar recyclers ranked by assets ('B' stands for Billion):

Norway Government Pension Fund:	$1073B
UAE Abu Dhabi Investment Authority:	$696 B
UAE Abu Dhabi Mubadala InvestCo:	$125 B
UAE Abu Dhabi Investment Council:	$123 B
UAE Emirates Investment Authority:	$34 B
Kuwait Investment Authority:	$592 B

Saudi Arabia SAMA:	$494 B
Saudi Arabia Public Investment Fund:	$224 B
Qatar Investment Authority:	$320 B
National Development Fund of Iran:	$91 B
Russia National Welfare Fund:	$66.3 B
Alaska Permanent Fund:	$61.5 B
Kazakhstan Samruk-Kazyna:	$60.9 B
Kazakhstan National Fund:	$57.9 B
Brunei Investment Agency:	$40 B
Texas Permanent School Fund:	$37.7 B
Azerbaijan State Oil Fund:	$33.1 B

The amounts above change constantly and are mentioned to be indicative of the huge number of US PetroDollars ploughed into the world economy.

§8. US Dollar today – No easy way out

Current issues with the US Dollar are a result of the self-compensatory nature of markets. That which is desired but is not available is valued, while as availability increases value decreases.

Having been the measure, scale and unit of the world economy, US Dollar had the capability to be weaponized. As long as was not weaponized, it had the advantage of deterrence. In the last few years US has used currency as a weapon, thereby scaring all nations – friends and foes of US alike - of US economic hegemony. Candidly-said, unjustified, sudden, whimsical changes in international relations and sanctions on use of the SWIFT transaction system and obstruction in free flow of US Dollars for nations perceived hostile to US has left allies of US more worried than foes because using an alternative system of accounting and exchanging value amongst foes is natural anywhere in the world, as an enemy is expected to do whatsoever he can to protect his interests. But it is the friends that are hit hard. They cannot suddenly behave like foes. They are deprived of abilities for self-protection as they heavily depend on the hegemon and may be forced to comply with any whimsical, unanticipated demand or order. An example is US insistence for EU's and other US friendly nations' curbing their trade with Iran when the Trump regime reneged on the Iran nuclear deal (JCPOA) signed by the previous American administration and five other nations and ratified by the United Nations

This has motivated various groups all over the world to explore economic schemes and avenues to reduce US monetary hegemony without causing mayhem on the markets or in the value of the US Dollar, which constitutes forex reserves of these very nations. Various ideas came up. Some, including cryto-currencies, have been tried by Venezuela. But success has eluded those endeavours so far.

8.1. Reasons for pole position of US Dollar
There are many reasons for US & US Dollar being in a pole position.

8.1.1. Barring a few years (1954, 1958, 1974, 1975, 1980, 1982, 1991, 2008-09) the US Economy expanded post-WWII at an average rate of 3.22% p.a. Starting with a real GDP of US$2.29 trillion in 1950, US economy has expanded to US$19 trillion in 2019 (not taking into account the real devaluation of the greenback that would have occurred had the US Dollars not been exported). In 2019 US accounted for 15.11% of the world GDP. US accounts for 18% of world trade in imports and 14% in exports. These percentages are decreasing constantly since the seventies but remain very high in absolute figures.

8.1.2. The US is happy running a large current account (hereinafter CA) deficit starting from US$2.62Billion in 1970, the early petrodollar year, peaking all the way to ~US$806billion in 2005 and since the year 2010 it is maintained at ~US$430Billion annually. What this means is that this is the amount of US

Dollars that are printed annually and exported to nations all around the world. None other than US have the capacity or will to run humungous CA deficits.

8.1.3. Add to it that US has the largest external and internal debt among large nations at US$23.30 trillion (~76% of the GDP) and about 29% of this debt is owned by foreigners. The United States has the largest external debt in the world. Easy credit and high debt ensured huge consumption rates and a non-inflationary growth for US economy through export of the currency abroad. US Dollars (US Promises of delivering value at prevalent rates, whenever these US Dollars are produced to procure goods and services from US) printed and shipped abroad are used to purchase and import goods and services from all over the world. To sustain gargantuan US domestic consumption levels, the level of public debt is raised constantly along with provision of easy credit to fuel the high consumption of average Americans, who constitute 5% of the world's population but consume 24% of the world's energy. Household expenditure per capita in US stands at ~38 thousand US Dollars. Amongst countries with more than 100 million people (disregarding smaller nations countries to make sensible comparisons), Japan follows US with an annual per capita household US$20'000 which is almost half of American; followed by Russia at US$13'000; Brazil at

US$8'000, Indonesia at US$5'645; China at US$5'548; Philippines at US$5364; India at ~US$4'000. The US, therefore stands far above all other big nations in terms of its per capita household expenditure. This ensures that factories and services providers in China, India, Vietnam, Bangladesh etc. remain operational.

8.1.4. Of total reserves held by IMF member countries (calculated in US Dollar equivalents) US Dollars accounts for US$6,617 billion ; Euros - 2,219 billion US$ worth; Japanese Yen 558 billion US$ worth; British Pounds 475 billion US$ worth; Canadian Dollars 197 billion US$ worth; Australian Dollars 174 billion US$ worth; Chinese RMB 202 billion US$ worth. Therefore, to date US Dollars account for 63% of the aforementioned global reserves.

8.1.5. Conclusion: Any fall in the value of US Dollar provoked by any of the nations that hold US debt and currency will take the international economy into a tailspin, escaping control of any one or group of nations.

It is apparent that there is no magic wand to make the system more equitable by freeing from US Dollar hegemony. Removing the US Dollar from its pole position through administrative means engineered by those opposed to US financial hegemony is not feasible. The way back to equity among all nations is a long one and no mechanisms that defy fundamental economic logic will have a positive impact.

The economic state that the world found itself in was one in which major producing nations wanted a large buyer ready to buy even if on credit. America elected to be that buyer and the largest debtor in world history. **Asset** Sellers to America, prospered in (i) US promises (currency); (ii) resources that could be bought from third nations because US promises (US Dollars) were acceptable to most, thanks to the Bretton Woods and Petro-dollar arrangement, consequently causing a mere transfer of US promises from one donor to another; (iii) rising US debt that kept on boosting per capita household consumption by leaps and bounds to absorb a colossal inflow of goods and services against the export of currency and debt.

8.2. So where are we today?

- The US Dollar is the major most reserve currency, which means that nations executing transactions and earning in various currencies prefer to convert these currencies into US Dollars.

- The US Dollar is also the base currency for all currency exchanges. Therefore, when a Rupee's value is to be assessed in terms of Rubles, it is done through Ruble's value to US Dollar and Rupee's value to US Dollar. There is no market price for settling Rupees against Rubles or vice-versa.

China along with Hong Kong has the largest US Dollar reserves (close to 4 trillion) followed by India, Brazil, Germany. Russia on the other hand has in the last two years substantially reduced the proportion of US Dollars in its forex reserves.

Post Nixon shock, every US Dollar is backed by nothing but a promise (the famous 'full faith and credit of the US Government') to either give another Dollar in return or let the holder buy as many goods and/or services as any US supplier may be ready to deliver for a US Dollar and subject to whatever are the prevalent export control mechanisms of the US Government!

§9. The Base Currency

Technically, there could be (i) political / geo-political / regulator driven reasons or (ii) Market driven economic reasons for the existence of a base currency.

Often the former reasons are used for creation of later and they drive economics thereafter. This has been so in case of US Dollar. The Bretton Woods Agreement followed by Petro-Dollar arrangements of US with the Middle-East led to use of US Dollar as the base currency for exchange rates.

It also needs to be mentioned that when the global economic order came into being the technological level of mankind was very different from the present one. A pertinent question that arises then is that while technology has impacted every walk of human life, why is the global economic system of 1950s still surviving? The reason apparently is geo-political.

9.1. US Dollar – its percolation

The largest seven traded currencies (titled 'Majors') in the world are all traded against US Dollar:

- E.U.'s Euro versus the U.S. Dollar: EUR/USD - 27% of daily currency trade
- U.S. Dollar versus the Japanese Yen: USD/JPY – 13% of daily currency trade
- U.K.'s Pound Sterling versus the U.S. Dollar: GBP/USD – 13% of daily currency trade
- U.S. Dollar versus the Swiss Franc: USD/CHF – 5% of daily currency trade
- Australian Dollar versus the U.S. Dollar: AUD/USD

- U.S. Dollar versus the Canadian Dollar: USD/CAD
- New Zealand Dollar versus the U.S. Dollar: NZD/USD

Once the US Dollar was elevated to the prime position replacing the British Pound, the US could propagate a virtuous cycle that kept the American economy strong, supporting the value of US Dollar and making it the most powerful currency, globally. Around $580 billion in U.S. bills (physical currency) are used outside the country that is 65% of all dollars in circulation. That includes 75% of $100 bills, 55% of $50 bills, and 60%of $20 bills. Most of these bills are in the former Soviet Union member countries and Latin America. They serve as a non-inflationary currency in nations that suffer high or hyper-inflation. The US Dollar is a refuge for savings in such politically and economically unstable countries.

Besides cash US Dollars in circulation, more than one-third of the world's gross domestic product comes from countries that peg their currencies to the dollar. That includes seven countries that have adopted the US Dollar as their own. Another 89 countries keep their currency in a tight trading range relative to the Dollar.

In the foreign exchange market, the US Dollar rules. Around 90% of forex trading involves US Dollars. The US Dollar is one of the world's 185 currencies but most of these currencies are only used inside their own countries.

Theoretically, any one of them could replace the US Dollar as world's currency, but they won't because they aren't as widely traded. Below-mentioned is a breakdown of 10 most traded currencies in 2018. The percentages reflected below are calculated as number of trade transactions of each of the mentioned currencies versus all currency transactions. Each currency transaction involves any one of the below-mentioned currency vis-à-vis any one of the remainder in the list below.

US Dollars	90.00%
Euro	31.00%
Japanese Yen	21.00%
British Pound	12.00%
Australian Dollar	07.00%
Canadian Dollar	05.00%
Swiss Franc	05.00%
Chinese Yuan	04.00%
Swedish Kronas	02.20%
Mexican Peso	02.20%

Example – if there were a total of 100 transactions, then 90 of those transactions will have US Dollar as being one currency while the other currency in the transaction could be one of the remainder nine.

9.2. US Dollar and Global Debt

Issue of 40% of world's debt in US Dollars results in Non-US Banks demanding a lot of Dollars to conduct business. This became evident during the 2008 financial crisis. Non-American banks had US$27 trillion in international liabilities denominated in foreign currencies. Out of that, $18 trillion was in U.S. Dollars. Hence, the U.S. Federal Reserve had to increase its Dollar swap line. That was the only way to keep the world's banks from running out of dollars.

The financial crisis made the Dollar even more widely used. In 2017, the banks of Japan, Germany, France, and the UK held more liabilities denominated in US Dollars than in their own currencies.

Additionally, bank regulations enacted to prevent another crisis have made dollars scarce, and the Federal Reserve increased the fed funds rate. That decreases the money supply by making Dollars more expensive to borrow.

US Dollar's strength is the reason for it becoming the Base Currency and the one against which Majors as well as all other currencies have a market rate.

Some governments invest their reserves in foreign currencies. China and Japan deliberately buy the currencies of their main export partners. The United States is the largest export partner with both countries. They try to keep their currencies cheaper in comparison so their exports are competitively priced.

9.3. Calls for a One World Currency
In March 2009, China and Russia called for a new global currency.

They wanted the world to create a reserve currency "that is disconnected from individual nations and is able to remain stable in the long run, thus removing the inherent deficiencies caused by using credit-based national currencies."

China is concerned that the trillions it holds in dollars would be worthless if dollar inflation set in. This could happen as a result of increased U.S. deficit spending and printing of U.S. Treasury to support U.S. debt. China called for the International Monetary Fund to develop a currency to replace the dollar.

In the fourth quarter of 2016, the Chinese Renminbi became another one of the world's reserve currencies. As of the first quarter of 2019, the world's central banks held $213 billion worth, according to the IMF. That's a fraction of the $6.7 trillion held in U.S. dollars but henceforth, it will continue to grow. China wants its currency to be fully traded on the global foreign exchange markets. It would like the Yuan to replace the Dollar as the global currency. To do so, China is rapidly reforming its economy.

9.4. US Dollar Strength - The Bottom Line

Despite trillions of debt and ever larger deficit spending, US still commands trust in its ability to provide value for its promises. U.S. Dollar, therefore, remains the strongest as well as the Base Currency. It may continue to be the top global currency for some years to come.

§10. The Pegged and the Sliding

All Central Banks (Reserve or Federal Banks) other than the US Federal Reserve do interventions (sell or buy US Dollars in their reserves) to maintain a trend of the national currency vis-à-vis US Dollar. As of now there are two trends:

10.1. Pegging

Pegging is nailing rigidly one's currency to US Dollar. This is done by nations with a major trade proficit (surplus) vis-à-vis US that are keen to maintain the proficit. Large proficits would generally lead to appreciation of the Nation's (US Counterparty') currency vis-à-vis US Dollar. This makes the cost of goods and services exported to US more expensive for people there and hence the produce less competitive for exports (as in case of China) and it discourages local production & encourages imports (as in the case of UAE or Saudi Arabia which has maintained the exchange rate of a US Dollar to Riyal at 3.75 for more than a decade).   To maintain high levels of trade proficit (surplus) the central banks of these nations keep on purchasing all those amount of US Dollars that are in surplus to maintain the exchange rate nailed or pegged to US Dollar. In the seesaw equivalent, more and more US Dollars added to the market should have led to a slide of the fulcrum towards the US Dollar (that is a reduction of US Dollar rate vis-à-vis Counterparty's) to maintain the balance.

But what the State (Chinese) did is – every time extra US Dollars turn up on the seesaw, exceeding the demand, the

State picks them up in sufficient amount to ensure that the fulcrum need not be moved (hence the rate of US Dollars) at all to keep the seesaw in air.

China did this successfully for 2 decades, which led to ballooning of their US Dollar reserves to 4 trillion (including Hong Kong). Pegging therefore, led to unprecedented accumulation of US Dollars in Chinese Forex Reserves.

The Chinese actually found for themselves a complementing position to US economic doctrine and therefore rode the wave along with US for last few decades.

US Government printed & exported US Dollars, got consumables in return, which were used to raise consumption and credit was provided internally to ensure the consumption went up without deflation in product prices resulting in market collapse. The Chinese complemented that policy - they manufactured & exported large volumes of goods & services for the burgeoning US Consumption, kept on sucking US Dollars out of their markets into their reserves to keep the trade balance up. The extraordinary amounts of Yuans released in domestic Chinese market were used for exporting further and building infrastructure, more than what was needed. Generally, in free markets, over-supply of infrastructure (roads, bridges, housing etc.) would have led to diminishing of revenues (tolls and housing costs) leading to incapability of the borrowers to service their debt – leading to NPAs (Non-performing asset). But not so in China, where bad loans are evergreened (newer loans are given by banks to borrowers to pay instalments of existing loans, thereby keeping the accounts functional and performing). Therefore, as is evident from aforementioned data, the tentacles of this global financial pyramid have penetrated deep. And the rot could commence the domino effect from any agent/participant of the food chain.

The pyramid scheme worked well for many years but the 2008 crisis and the consequent follow-up made the Chinese authorities sceptical about the continuing viability of the system. There were calls by Russia and China both to change the global currency regime. When these met with no success, the Chinese decided to use their accumulated US Dollars to buy fixed assets in the US. However out of strategic and national security concerns, US stonewalled Chinese investments. This is when the quite, but smart, Chinese came up with 'OBOR', later BRI (Belt and Road Initiative).

On thorough study I discovered the interesting fact that decline in Chinese investment in US coincides with adoption of OBOR as a Chinese strategic objective. After Chinese FDI in the United States hit its peak of $46 billion in 2016, the number fell to $29 billion the following year. According to a Rhodium Group report Chinese acquisitions and green-field investment in the United States from January to May of 2018 clocked only $1.8 billion, the lowest net value in seven years. In addition to investing far less in the face of US government opposition, Chinese companies are also divesting at an unprecedented rate, putting their existing foreign assets, such as real estate holdings up for sale.

To rid themselves of the US Dollar reserves substantially, while gaining strategic depth in the global supply chain, the Chinese leaders devised the OBOR/BRI project, through which they intend to invest the accumulated Dollars in nations around the world, thereby using these Dollars to buy fixed assets globally. It is the Chinese Marshal Plan at a Chinese scale.

Investments in accumulated US Dollars are prudently mixed with Yuans, such that not only do they get rid of extra, unnecessarily stockpiled US Dollars by placing them in other nations, where they purchase or long lease fixed assets, while simultaneously injecting Yuans and making them internationally acceptable. US Dollars injected in these economies, will end up back in US or will get spread amongst numerous nations of the world.

OBOR, is a smart Chinese way to not only enhance their global stature and reach, but also circumvent the American investment Wall. US, in this case, can do very little except try to discredit the concept and pressure other states not to participate.

10.2. Sliding

Sliding currencies are those which are less competitive in exports. India is a glaring example. Indian manufacturers never reached Chinese exports levels but for the IT sector. In economies of scale they could not match the Chinese and never became export economies like the PRC, South Korea and other Asian manufacturing giants. To compensate countries like India, have been depreciating their currency vis-à-vis US Dollar constantly for the last few decades. Thereby, they have survived as players, but have not raised their profiles in manufacturing. It is interesting to compare (study the difference) between the American and Chinese respective quests for technology, which the media are often compares.

A quick glance on publicly available data shows a gravitational difference in this regard between the two giants. US innovates because it is an inalienable, innate aspect of its technopreneurial culture, China on the other hand needs technology to keep its export driven economy fired. Like most Asians (Japanese, Taiwanese & South Koreans included) both Chinese and Indians are resistant to innovations, culturally. All Asian nations have a strict code of respect that starts within the family. 'Agyakarita' (obedience in Hindi) is a great virtue in all Asian cultures. It breeds antipathy to intellectual and cultural rebellion and change. Such cultures are not suitable cradles for creating innovation driven nations. Having said that, India and China are both undergoing great cultural churns. So the said situation might change in the coming few decades and many Chinese as well as Indians are proving far more inventive and forward looking than they used to be, though the proportions of such people are grossly sub-critical for a renaissance.

Nonetheless, it is apparent that the Chinese quest for technology is driven largely by the need to compete with innovative products in US and Europe and to sustain an export driven economy. There still is little to nothing that is invented from scratch in China without precedent in other parts of the world or something that is not an improvement on that which is already invented in the west (especially US).

So, India and many others, which could not become factories for the world, devalue (slide) their currency perennially.

There is a false belief among many economists in India that endlessly devaluing the currency is the way to boost exports. What is surprising is the insistence of many mainstream Indian economists that there are 'other' reasons, besides the monetary one for constant failure of this theory, for the last twenty-five years. They spend all their time looking for these other reasons, so as not to look in face the abject failure of India on the exports front despite a sliding Rupee. In truth, devaluing the currency, obstructs FDI (Foreign Direct Investment), because the investor has to plan to ensure that dividends, which he desires to ultimately take to his country of origin are constantly adjusted for loss in the local currency's value. This grossly discourages investment. With investment much below the required levels, there are fewer new jobs leading to what has been termed as 'jobless growth' by erstwhile Prime Minister of India Dr.Manmohan Singh. Therefore, consumption growth remains sluggish. To counter this effect, it is important to reduce the cost of capital, stabilise the Indian Rupee and completely remove any barriers to Foreign & Domestic Investment. A stable currency will lead to more investment in large long-term projects, cheaper capital, a rise in economies of scale and large exports.

We don't advocate pegging the Rupee rigidly to a US Dollar (said strategy is now too old and known for its perils caused to US, to work), but make sure that the Rupee behaves very stably.

I have no doubts that Indian traders have the ability to take over the world, once they get access to global scale sourcing within India.

§11. How did it come to this?

The entire world has hoarded US Dollars not because it was a premise for a specific economic model or because the US was happy with the consequences of this hoarding), but by virtue of

- Nations blindly following each other;
- geo-politics creating conducive market conditions
- lack of application of mind and a laissez affaire approach to the global economy;
- US technological and military dominance.

"The World is splendidly positioned for a Black Swan event."

Such an event might be triggered by completely disconnected events, which might seem controllable and possibly unlinked to exchange rates. The most likely cause of such a historical cascade is going to be an international dispute of some kind or a calamity (force majeure) such as the Covid-19 pandemic of 2019-2020.

The prevailing situation gives the US Dollar an unprecedented leverage over all other currencies because of an international demand created by third countries, which use it to trade amongst themselves. That endows the US with an immense capability to procure & consume goods from all around the world without causing inflation at home. Brazil and China use US Dollars to trade in goods that are neither purchased not sold in the US. The use of US Dollars in Trade & commerce have made it mandatory to hold US

Dollar currency reserves. The Petro-dollar further increased the need for US Dollars. This created a self-perpetuating loop favourable to the American currency, the more the world traded (even without US either selling or buying), the more the world needed US Dollars, thus enhancing the need for importing them as investment, remittances, strategic or speculative reserves and through trade.

This ensured a lion's share for United States in international trade. Per capita consumption of goods in US also went up in tandem. Easy consumer credit for Americans ensured consumption kept pace with influx of goods and services against exported promises (US Dollars).

11.1. Can India-Russia or EU-India create a separate currency swap mechanism circumventing US Dollar?

Creating exchange rates distinct from the ones available on world markets seems to yield no quality solution. A currency swap only enables the nations swapping currencies to create a reserve of each-others' currency, thereby enabling conduction of correspondent relations through their respective Banks. But the said system is sub-optimal as it requires invoicing in the Seller nation's currency. If an Indian Company is buying goods from a Russian Company it will have to buy Russian Rubles against payment in Indian Rupees. Furthermore, the purchase of Russian Rubles will be done by dividing the US Dollar-to-Ruble rate with the US Dollar-to-Indian Rupee rate. On the face of it, it seems that for the Companies there is no other calculable risk, because the transaction is done at the prevalent rate calculated by dividing Ruble-US$ by INR-US$ rate. However, the gains/losses[9] are actually transferred to the Banks or further back to the Governments which swap and store each others' currencies. Here is an example – Had Russia swapped Rubles @70/US$ in 2018 for a year, the reverse swap would have had to be done at a completely different rate to ensure no loss was incurred to either country in US Dollars. This needs to be done in a pre-determined manner owing to something called opportunity cost of capital, which means that an economic agent with currency in possession would invest in the instrument which would yield the highest returns. In case the agent is coerced into buying or selling a specific asset, it will lead to loss or a gain depending on the movement of rates.

Two concurrent systems, therefore, will not survive. There are three possible components that will determine the exchange rate in an ideal world between Russia and India and say similarly between Russia and US (exchange of all physical, intangible and financial assets) – Trade, Remittances, Investment, Reserves (strategic + speculative), Exchange-Entropy (explained ahead in this paragraph).

Say the exchange rate ascertained by the first 4 components is 1:1 between Ruble and Rupee. Now let us assume that the US Dollar & Rubles exchange rate determined by Russo-American Trade is 1 : 1.2 in favour of the Rupee, while that of USD : INR is 1 : 1.1 in favour of the Ruble. In such a

---

[9]One of the two sides is bound to lose and the other to gain depending on how the US$ to INR rate moves vis-à-vis US$ to Ruble rate.

situation it will become more profitable to first convert RUB into USD and USD into INR than to convert RUB directly into INR. This routing could be achieved through multiple steps and multiple intermediate currencies, until the optimal output is achieved. Such currency movement will therefore, impact the exchange rates, till an equilibrium is achieved. Hence, I term it Exchange-Entropy.

Therefore, any exchange rate that is artificially established leads to skewed benefits in favour of one or the other party; in the prevailing circumstances it is the US, in another situation it could be Russia or India or indeed the US in a Russia-India relationship. Therefore, for a fair exchange rate it is crucial to have convertibility & openness.

Nevertheless, this convertibility and openness is not possible for multiple politico-economic reasons, which are very different for each nation. Hence, these circumstances are not the subject matter of this paper. Owing to lack of open & free convertibility for all currencies, the system will look to a single or a set of reference currencies (principally contributing to the world trade) for setting a heuristic exchange rate. In many less stable nations and currencies the process is further skewed. Imports are apparently paid in US Dollars, but even for exports the proceeds are retained in US Dollars, owing to the instability of the local currency. This is a double whammy for the economy of a nation. The US Dollar for multiple reasons, therefore automatically dominates. Indeed, notwithstanding a strong desire of many countries to jointly dethrone the US Dollar (Russia and

China both have been at it for some time) from the pole position, they are not being able to find a suitable mechanism because, any such mechanism – say some kind of special drawing rights with BRICS Bank, will end up getting benchmarked to the US Dollar, thereby using the US Dollar as an indirect base currency rather than a direct one. This is damaging, as whenever the conversions are indirect, there is an associated higher cost that is levied on transitory transactions causing frictional, circulation losses. An example – If Rubles are converted into Rupees and then into US Dollars, there are two exchange risk exposures and two conversion costs as against Rubles being directly converted into US Dollars.

Another example: Let's assume that some SDRs (Special Drawing Rights) are introduced by BRICS, Russia and India start accepting goods invoiced in such SDRs. If for any business, Rupee to SDR & SDR to RUB is going to be more expensive than INR to USD and USD to RUB, traders will quickly opt for the latter; leading thereby to discovery of the SDR to USD exchange rate through sale-purchase of USD & SDRs to annul the arbitrage.

There is also a critical geo-political angle to this problem. Any/all nations, which create and pose a threat to US Dollar domination will have to bear the wrath of world's largest trader and investor. This makes the process all the more difficult and painful for both the US and its partners – essentially China, Russia, Europe, Latin America and India.

A similar problem (though in reverse) existed post World War II, when US was in proficit vis-à-vis all European Nations. To provide US Dollars in the hands of Europeans grants were provided under Marshall Plan.

Unfortunately for the US, the main rivals this time are not Europeans with whom culturally and politically America can identify with and trust easily. This time they are China, Russia, Japan, India, Brazil and Saudi Arabia amongst others. India and to lesser extent Brazil are somewhat politically and culturally close to the US. China and Russia on the other hand have political systems and cultural traditions that that do not inspire confidence in the US, which sees itself as the champion of the Judaeo-Christian anglo-saxon heritage.

§12. Way forward

Any currency exchange mechanism established to circumvent US Dollar as Base Currency is, as we have explained theoretically difficult to realize, in view of US being the largest trader of goods/services, investments, reserves and largest beneficiary of Exchange-Entropy[10] induced financial movements. Any mechanism created to trump the US Dollar is doomed to fail or not grow to any sensible proportion as it leaves the root cause (described in the workflow) unaddressed.

Additionally, when it comes to INR-RUB trade, any exchange rate that is set circumventing the US Dollar, leads to a run for rerouting of trade and currencies through the beneficial route, whichever is going to be optimal for the traders.

Additionally, any mechanism that damages the US Economy will devalue the holdings of the creditors of United States – China, Russia, India, EU, Japan and Brazil among others.

So what is the way out before a war to end American dominance is fought not with weapons, but by destroying the US currency, even if it comes at a cost to holders of US Dollars, who might end up partly compromising their own

---

[10]Say the exchange rate ascertained by the first 4 components is 1:1 amongst Ruble and Rupee. Now let's assume, that the US Dollar & Ruble exchange rate determined by Russo-American Trade is 1:1.2 in favour of India, while that of USD:INR is 1:1.1 in favour of Ruble. In such a situation it will become more profitable to first convert RUB into USD and USD into INR than to convert RUB directly into INR. This routing could be achieved through multiple routing, till the optimal result is achieved. Such currency movement will therefore impact the exchange rates, till an equilibrium is achieved. Hence, I termed it Exchange-Entropy.

economic security with such an action, yet be forced to execute it. It is important to note that nations are not rational and often steep policies are guided by national pride rather than economic interests.

I think the democratic world has to join hands to ensure that the US Economy and as a consequence the global economy does not fail nor does the US Dollar. India could lead the charge.

12.1. Does US care about the magnitude of the problem facing the world ?

I believe so. While the economists have been warning us of a looming crisis for some time, yet the policy makers were busy projecting current good times into better ones in the future and avoided questioning the sustainability of the pyramid that the world economy created by using the US as a buyer, whose unlimited resources are created by constantly raising its national debt.

President Donald Trump seems to have gauged the scope of the problem. Hence, not without reason, is US encouraging production and investment domestically. The way back to stability in the world economy is for the US to produce more competitively priced goods and services in America and to export them in sufficient volumes to ensure that a balance is restored between imports and exports.

At the high labour costs in the US, it could not hope to be a competitive manufacturing hub, but now thanks to digitization, automation and robotization of manufacturing,

US does stand a serious chance again to become a source of high-end manufactured goods.

This indirectly means that purchase of fixed assets other than infrastructure (utilized by local Americans) seems not to augur well for foreign investors investing into America. The US Dollars held by entities globally, can be used in one's own country or third countries where said entity is making an investment by

(i)   buying services in US;

(ii)   fixed assets, which serve the people of America, mainly newly built infrastructure,

(iii)   Securities of companies that manufacture goods and services that are exported out of US (as this leads again to soaking of US Dollars abroad). Such investments will lead to higher growth in the US, boosting the domestic economy. Those holding US Dollars will have to invest in purchase of US Goods and invest in US fixed assets that will produce goods that can be exported from the US. US shall have to be made an export hub of sorts leading to another major spurt of economic growth in the country. Exceptionally high rates of automation would help to make this possible. Factually, the bid has to increase the denominator while keeping the nominator constant in order to achieve the desired proportion. This seems the only sensible and painless way for the global economy to sustain itself and avoid an economic war. Any other inorganic or disruptive attempt will carry unbearable cost in economic and military terms. In the new system the US will have to undergo some bearable pain as inflation might accompany growth of the American economic base further.

Depreciation of US Dollar vis-à-vis other currencies, will further spurt growth of investments into United States as the world will be able to buy more of US goods and assets at lower prices in their own currencies.

§13. Inspiration to create Indycia

Indycia was borne from the desire to find a solution that would yield benefits across next two decades. It is meant to spread slowly and cause no harm, especially to the United States. Ideally it has to be beneficial for the US in order to grow and last.

It was important to create a mechanism that would strain neither the US Dollar's value nor the US economy. Damage to any of these two would lead to damage to the value of the foreign exchange reserves against which resources have been exported from respective nations.

During the session on trade in national currencies amongst India and Russia, it was apparent that there is a desire amongst all the stakeholders to ensure that India creates a mechanism to work with its traditional ally irrespective of third party mood swings and strategic interference from Europe and America.

After attending the meeting, I felt that the scale and depth of the problem was understood by the participants, yet there was no clarity on how to solve it. Of course no one desires to jeopardise Indo-US relationship.

The next few months were spent thinking, trying various options and discarding them. Around this time Come Carpentier De Gourdon and myself joined hands to find a real, effective and implementable mechanism.

A few meetings with bureaucrats made it amply clear that not only did most not understand technology intensive solutions, but that they believe that anything to do with exchange rates and currencies is strictly in the purview of the Sovereign. Most such meetings with some important economists and bureaucrats yielded those conclusions.

Notwithstanding rare encouragement coming our way the very complexity of the issue was enticing. We felt that such a complex problem statement can have only an entrepreneurial solution. Owing to this condition India would not want to be even remotely seen to propose a solution that might pose a challenge to existing US Dollar based global trade arrangements.

For similar reasons, it is also clear that the existing large corporation with substantial balance sheets will not fit the bill to be solution provider. No large corporate would desire to see his current standing or businesses jeopardized because of a new unproven and geopolitically risky business. Everyone is invested in the established norms. This is the strength of such norms.

This implied that if at all a technological resolution to the stated problem is found it would come from a Startup, one which builds a business out of the proposed solution from scratch and has no large burgeoning balance sheet to keep and protect. Thus thought Zarathustra, "It's time and mine is the calling".

In the last few months, we designed Indycia to solve all the three problem statements articulated on previous pages. It is well understood that perfect solutions are a mirage. A solution that addresses 70% plus situations adequately should be implemented and adopted as satisfactory. In heuristics the perfect is the enemy of good. Perfect doesn't exist. 70% is good because when a majority of users adopt a solution, the minority to which the solution is not palatable for whatsoever reasons end up subsequently changing their habits and ways of doing business to work fruitfully within the altered/amended prevalent system.

A few months passed architecting the solution. The biggest challenge was to make the proposed instrument non-objectionable and ideally to present an attractive game plan for American interests to enable its execution.

§14. Description of Indycia as it should be designed

'Indycia', by AICORPS EPL is a blockchain-controlled product that engages with its subscribers to ensure all the attributes that have been enlisted in Section 11 of this Book.

The word Indycia is derived by modulating the root 'Indic' to give it a botanical (flowery) resonance.

14.1. Defining risks & their mitigation for Indycia

Possible risks to be addressed while designing Indycia:

14.1.1. Risk of Run on Money

All financial instruments are based on trust and the challenge they face is sudden run on the money creating a liquidity crisis, often owing to rumours.

14.1.2. Exchange Risk

14.1.2.1. This is the most critical risk that the instrument has to be protected from. Indeed, the popularity of the instrument shall be contingent on the extent to which the risks associated with the exchange of currency are mitigated.

14.1.2.2. Indycia has to be designed in a manner that completely evades US Dollar exchange rate risk.

14.1.3. Credit Risk

The risk that the issuer of the instrument won't have enough money to make interest payments or redeem the instrument at face value when such redemption (in whatever form and irrespective of how is it termed) is due. The higher the credit risk, the higher shall be the risk of default leading to payment of higher returns.

14.1.4. Inflation Risk

The risk of losing purchasing power. If the instrument gains 5% in a year and the cost of living goes up by 2%, one is left with a real return of only 3%.

14.1.5. Market Risk

The risk that one will lose some or all of the principals. As markets fluctuate, there is always a possibility that the instrument is caught in a decline.

14.1.6. Interest Risk

The risk that rising interest rates will cause the instrument to decline in value. When interest rates rise, instrument prices might decline and mutual funds may also decline as a result.

14.1.7. Other important risk mitigation measures

14.1.7.1. The risk that rising interest rates will cause the instrument to decline in value. When interest rates rise, instrument prices might decline and mutual funds may also decline as a result.

14.1.7.2. A top quality financial instrument that attracts premium investors, has to rate high on mitigation measures that are undertaken to ensure that the fundamentals of the instrument are strong.

14.1.7.3. Risk mitigation will be algorithmic and completely free of human intervention.

14.1.7.4. Liquidity of Indycia has to be exceptionally high, if not the highest in the industry.

14.2. Fitness attributes of Indycia

The necessary attributes of the instrument be invented are

14.2.1. Fitness for purpose attributes of Indycia

Fitness for purpose for which something is done is the most critical necessary condition that has to be fulfilled.

Some of the desired objectives are:

14.2.1.1. Enabling a mechanism for transferring value between any two entities of two separate nations without use of SWIFT or US Dollars as a medium of conversion and transfer of value. India-Russia trade is a case in point.

14.2.1.2. Working out a mechanism to create a market based Rupee-Ruble (just an example, the solution has to work for any two currencies) exchange rate that bypasses the US Dollar, if possible.

14.2.1.3. Making sure that the value of National reserves is not compromised through implementation of the solution. Nor should India's relationship with US should be soured by it.

14.2.1.4. The solution has to be sustainable. Else it will not be implementable by highly diverse nations – think about India, China, Brazil, South Africa and Russia – the BRICS – they are different in almost everything. Throw in Saudi Arabia and ASEAN and the rainbow is complete,

14.2.1.5. In the long run resolve the problem related to weaponization of US Dollar, in a manner that is painless for the US and for the world at large.

14.2.1.6. Along with a stated policy to benefit the United States of America's monetary system, it is pertinent to ensure that Indycia is protected from political interventions by the US and other G20 Governments. This is critically important, so that people are assured that their savings are beyond the reach of State Policy whims.

14.2.1.7. It is the endeavour of Indycia to pave the way for an equitable system of currency valuation and exchange that is not inclined to favour any economic agent. This indeed will lay the foundation for a free meritocratic market. An earnest attempt is being made to position Indycia as a globally acceptable Base for currency exchanges.

14.2.2. Description of time-fitness attributes of Indycia

The time-fitness attribute is to double-check that at the time of issuance of the instrument in the market it should not only be non-controversial, but optimal as well. Below are the facts that lead us us conclude that the time is ripe to offer a solution.

14.2.2.1. US's banning Companies from all nations from working with Iran, blocking Russian oil and gas giants from raising investment or investing in

Europe or US, thereby making it very difficult for India to work with its traditional Russian partners. Purchase of defence equipment that is connected directly with India's National Security is hampered by US sanctions on many strategic enterprises of Russia.

14.2.2.2. India and Russia have sought to create a mechanism of their own whereby trade in national currencies could take place. Indeed as I pointed out earlier my being a part of meetings discussing India-Russia trade in national currencies inspired the desire to come up with something like Indycia. The best that came to the minds of the two Governments was a currency-swap mechanism. But it seems that the hidden costs of currency swaps detailed in 11.1 (Can India-Russia or EU-India create a separate currency swap mechanism circumventing US Dollar?) have not been taken into account. Therefore, there is a requirement at the Intergovernmental level amongst the BRICS nations to devise an acceptable and viable mechanism for value exchange.

14.2.2.3. A concern has been expressed in some quarters in the Indian State about the weaponization of US Dollars and the possibility that it could be used against India much like it has been used against Russia, in case Indian policies do not fall in line with the desires of US, which is quite possible.

14.2.2.4. Export of US Dollars has created a debt pyramid that let US currency multiply and the US GDP grow without any inflation. Russia offloaded US Dollar Reserves in favour of Euros and Gold, but if China decides to follow suit with its 4 trillion forex reserves, it would put major pressure on the US Dollar in currency markets. While China might never do anything that jeopardizes the value of its reserves, yet markets operate on information - both real and perceptual. A black swan event might be triggered by an unreal or largely perceptual event throwing global markets out of their highly precarious balance. And the situation for such an event is ripe.

14.2.2.5. Any major event that leads to loss of confidence in the US Dollar will affect India profoundly in its economy, finances and democratic institutions. US stability is critical for both China and India though for different reasons, India's being more social and civilizational, while for China – the issue is largely economic & financial.

Keeping all the aforementioned in view, the time for Indycia seems to have come. .

14.2.3. Ambience-fitness attributes of Indycia

The geo-ambience[11] fitness attribute ensures that the Indycia project starts in the right location and in a conducive ambience.

14.2.3.1. We should identify the jurisdictions that are not suitable to host this new product. Since Indycia is being designed to ensure that it is also beneficial to US. Russia and China are not viable options, owing to the adversarial geopolitical relations they have with the US. Besides these two, there are six major economies, which have substantial trade with US, thus making the implementation of Indycia attractive. These are EU, Canada, Mexico, Japan, South Korea and India. Since South Korea and Japan are politically very closely aligned with US and dependent on it, these could be less than ideal locations. Though Japan has one unique feature – it is the most receptive major economy to crypto-currencies. Of the others, EU, Canada, Mexico and India. Mexico is not a financial major nor is it a high technology oriented economy. EU, Canada and India are perhaps the most suitable environments. India amongst these four (EU, Canada, India & Japan) is unique in that it is close to the US, Russia, China of which the latter is a major holder of US Dollars. Both Russia and China could be the best clients for Indycia. Amongst EU member-nations, Baltic States (Estonia, Latvia, Lithuania) are attractive owing to a special arrangement they have with US as front

---

[11]The geographical and/or physical location of an object, person, phenomenon or event and its environs (surrounding objects, people, conditions, phenomena and events).

line states for NATO and to their proficiency in Crypto and Cyber technologies, besides a favourable corporate tax regime.

14.2.3.2. Amongst the three above – EU, Japan, Canada, India; India has a major drawback, it is least developed as far as bureaucratic engagement (Ease of Doing Business) and has the most cumbersome legal system. Japan is not much better. Therefore, it can be concluded that the most suitable jurisdictions to launch Indycia in order of preference are the following three - EU (Baltics), Canada, Japan and India. India has been essentially included in the matrix as amongst the four it is the only one which is not politically forced as a member of the western bloc to tow the US line vis-à-vis Russia and China.

14.2.4. Cost-fitness attributes of Indycia

The cost of the proposed service (transaction costs) has to be exceptionally low (if not free), if the client base is massive in numbers. If the clientele is going to consist mostly of large entities or sovereign funds, the transaction costs can be higher as such clients will be large but highly limited in number.

14.3. Sufficiency attributes of Indycia

Sufficiency attributes are those that ensure that Indycia is not declassified as a fruitful resource. This resilience to declassification as a fruitful resource is established on four major parameters.

14.3.1. Resistivity of Indycia to declassification as a fruitful resource owing to quantitative changes

14.3.1.1. Assuming the product is created to meet its primary purposes listed above, the solution (Indycia) shall certainly be issued in substantially large volumes. Ideally, there should not be any major quantitative constraints to the product. But in case the design mandates one, it has to be large enough to maintain the usability of the product.

14.3.1.2. At some point it will be sensible to stop issuing Indycia and let them appreciate vis-à-vis all currencies. The amount of Indycia is not an issue as they are digital and infinitely divisible into ever smaller units. Appreciation of Indycia vis-à-vis all other currencies including US Dollar will ensure that the Indycia redemption obligations of the Company are gradually reduced, thereby ensuring that Indycia within a few years or a decade becomes the hardest known currency. The hardness of any currency can be defined as its capability to withstand the progressive amounts subjected to exchange with least variation in rate. As Indycia appreciates, the redemption capability of the Company issuing Indycia will rise progressively. Making Indycia sustainable in the long run.

14.3.1.3.   In energy efficiency contracts, the capital expenditure is funded against the energy that will be saved because of the capital expenditure incurred.

14.3.1.4.   Similarly, in most USD to Indycia conversions the efficacy of transactions is enhanced in such a manner that transaction efficiency itself provides some sensible return through the year. Every Dollar undergoes loss through its traversal-like friction consuming tyres through drive. The friction in case of Indycia is absent (or theoretically negligible), hence the higher efficiency will get translated into return. The zero-return on holding conventional fiat (US Dollar) without employing it, also is a part of this loss on returns.

14.3.1.5.   Once, the Indycia is prevalent and new issues of Indycia will cease all that will be needed is to keep on dividing 'Indies' appropriately if and when their value goes up substantially. One could start with MilliIndycia and then go to MicroIndycia and NanoIndycia, as would be required; such a facility will be made available in the initial algorithm. The aim is to completely abolish the absolute value of Indycia by making it an instrument for measuring one's currency vis-à-vis all others and eliminating the need of US Dollar to enact this role. Indycia will be nothing but a multilateral, market-owned and managed international fiat, beyond control of any one Government.

14.3.2. Resistivity of Indycia to declassification as a fruitful resource owing to qualitative and property changes

14.3.2.1. Goodwill for a financial instrument largely exhibits its strength. A financial instruments' strength varies through time and therefore it is important to establish constraints and exclusions. Since Indycia (platform/instrument) will be made to let people handle their money using the provided technology, it has to be exceptionally high on transparency, easy to understand, should have lower constraints to avoid reduction of value of users' money. Indycia should take good advantage of existing networks including those of Banks to co-opt them rather than fight them.

14.3.2.2. In the current financial situation after the 2008 crisis in US the ongoing crisis of trust and misgivings about Banking has led to a shift of public desire from seeking higher returns to lowering risks. Therefore, higher transparency and risk aversion will be rewarded by users in preference to promises of large returns. Therefore, for success in the market, Indycia has to be exceptionally high on persistence of low risk profile, which must be inherent and embedded in the design of the instrument/product.

14.3.2.3.   One of the most important aspects of Indycia's properties that should not lend itself to change is the possibility of using the instrument to invest, produce and import from US such that the American economy grows, while the promises that US has provided the world over showcase a reversing trend. India is uniquely positioned to make this reversal happen, as it is a US strategic partner and investments from India will be welcomed there. Simultaneously, Indycia has to be designed to ensure that it reverses the trend of providing US Trade Overdrafts, resulting in the colossal deficits that US has been running for several decades.

14.3.2.4.   Since Indycia is being designed to be akin to a self-executing smart contract it should have built-in triggers to change form and property to maintain its resistivity to declassification as a fruitful resource. This will make Indycia highly resistant to risks, even if it comes at a cost of lack of attractiveness for high return seeking investors.

14.3.2.5.   To ensure high degree of transparency, immutability and exceptionally high resilience to hacking, Indycia is designed as a block-chain like product, while circumventing the major challenges that Companies face with block-chains, currently.

14.3.2.6.   It is important to ensure that there is no damage to US Dollar, it should indeed be designed to save and nurture the US Dollar causing no challenge or damage to its value and through it to the reserves of G20 Nations.

14.3.2.7.   Although designed as a block-chain, Indycia is not designed to be a crypto-currency. Nonetheless, Indycia is a digital asset (token) which is digitally and easily transferable. Nonetheless, it should be well understood that any digital asset, owing to ease of transfer and quickness in recognition can become currency-like. For instance Sodexo coupons became a fiat for grocery purchases since most large-chains accept them in India and most large Companies offer them to their employees as perquisites, owing to the tax advantage entailed by the use of Sodexo Coupons. Therefore, the Company issuing Indycia in no way controls Indycia's use profile. Users can end up using them for various purposes.

14.3.2.8.   Most important of all – Indycia shall be owned and controlled by the users collectively, and managed through a publicly open and transparent Trust which will operate digitally with an electronically user-elected Board.

100% of any and all profits shall belong completely to the subscribers of Indycia.

14.3.2.9. In case users start using Indycia for various purposes including transfer of value to each other, the system will lead to merit based economics, where prosperity and consumption will not happen for exchange of printable fiat or political influence and supremacy.

14.3.2.10. Indycia based system will be designed to ensure that no one can peg his currency against any other currency for fraudulently accrued gains. Any such pegging will lead to a distortion, whereby the cost of Indycia will rise, making the peg unsustainable.

14.3.2.11. The most important element that will allow the creation of a transparent system through the use of Indycia is that the consumers themselves will be using them. Since, Indycia will not be issued by any Government, until certain pre-determined criteria are fulfilled, and the Government will, if at all, act as another economic agent. It will lose the power to mismanage the economy by over-printing of currency.

14.3.2.12. Balanced growth (with no major spikes in current account deficit) will not impact the rate of a currency against an Indycia.

14.3.2.13. The more are Indycia demanded for settlement, the less will the US be able to boost consumption without generating inflation.

14.3.2.14. India's GDP in dollar terms will also rise substantially, as Indycia may give it a steroidal push.

14.3.2.15. There will be huge benefits for India to become the prime t mover of Indycia. It can retain the power to control the mechanism as it is the only very large country which enjoys an overall positive image in US financial circles.

14.3.2.16. A realistic exchange rate of various currencies will be established, thereby ensuring that the tendency of nations to trade with US because of the need for US Dollar as the medium of exchange will be reduced.

14.3.2.17. Indycia will promote higher merit based trade as the real advantages of nations like India with both knowledge and labour will automatically emerge.

14.3.2.18. Hopefully, in 30 years India could a global economic leader by following the monetary strategy for which Indycia lays the ground.

14.3.2.19. Indycia, I believe, will expand even faster than predicted owing to political circumstances which are here to stay irrespective of who is in power in United States or in India or Russia and China.

14.3.2.20.   More and more nations will desire to detoxify their economies by switching from regulated & manipulated US Dollars to deregulated, truly market governed digital Indycia.

14.3.2.21.   Carefully managing this transformational process can trigger India's rise to the top of world's economic pyramid.

14.3.2.22.   Attitude towards Product creation: The product has to ensure that the user gets a highly transparent tool to work with. Nothing should be left undisclosed.

14.3.2.23.   Voting: A voting mechanism has to be created for decisions to be taken in a justifiable manner. While scope has been left for more altruistic voting mechanisms that have been invented by Indycia, yet the default as of now is that of one Indycia being equal to one vote. Change in the voting mechanism has also to be executed using prevalent voting mechanism at the time of such a proposed change. The proposals put to voting will be the prerogative of the Management.

14.3.2.24.   Message: A messaging facility should be incorporated into the system– for customers to exchange and for the management to broadcast information.

14.3.3. Resistivity of Indycia to declassification as a fruitful resource owing to geo-ambience changes

14.3.3.1. The geo-ambience is of critical relevance. Design of Indycia has to take account of the competing products available in the market while ensuring that the product is available and legal in G20 nations including – EU, Argentina, Australia, Brazil, Canada, China, Germany, France, India, Indonesia, Italy, Japan, Mexico, the Russian Federation, Saudi Arabia, South Africa, South Korea, Turkey, the UK and the US in terms of jurisdictional validity. Its acceptance in the major US Dollar reserve holding countries (China + HK, India, Russia, Saudi Arabia, UAE, Japan, South Korea, EU, Taiwan) is a must for its success.

14.3.4. Resistivity of Indycia to declassification as a fruitful resource owing to ownership changes

14.3.4.1. The design of Indycia has to be such that it ensures transparency in the transfer of ownership, while access is fully protected for individual clients.

14.3.4.2. Indycia shall have its own marketplace for easy sale-purchase and execution of various conversions that Indycia might need. The marketplace will have no price discovery costs, while transaction costs will be negligible.

14.3.4.3. Individual rights shall be given precedence over collective ones, letting the users choose the risk profile for themselves through the use of Indycia for various operations.

14.3.4.4. Indycia could be widely held by autonomous large Financial Institutions with the undersigned being the project leader and being provided some sweat equity and a chairman's position with a recognition as the inventor and founder of the said technology & AICORPS EPL. The initial contributors will be allowed to guide and shape the investment policy. Indycia is built to automatically govern itself and its own issuance, with overriding powers to the shareholders/voters.

14.3.4.5. A secondary market for Indycia will be allowed, as the premium will reflect the trust & goodwill for the Indycia issuing Company.

14.4. Emotional Connect attributes of Indycia
14.4.1. Emotional Connect of the user

14.4.1.1. Since Indycia is designed as an instrument for mass use, its interface has to be exceptionally simple. Ease of use shall determine the success of the instrument.

14.4.1.2. It is equally important at some stage to embed technical facilities for the product to be accessible to the disabled (especially, blind, deaf and dumb) to operate the instrument.

14.4.1.3. Ux-Ui: All processes have to be fully automated. Automation means that the user should only be asked to buy or sell with a reconfirmation, besides which the user should not be asked to do anything. The critical information that is required for the user to make a final decision has to be made available to him or her on the very screen where he 'Okays' the transaction. So that each of decision taken is an informed decision.

14.5. Aesthetic Value of Indycia

The aesthetic value of Indycia shall be defined by the ease of use, which implies a conservative and intuitional design and operating mechanism,

§15. A window in Paris

'A window in Paris' is a Russian Comedy, where a family in St. Petersburg, suddenly discovers that by jumping out of one of the flat's windows, one instantaneously reaches another apartment in Paris. Neo-economists desire to avail of such quantum jumps for their economies, believing that technology is giving birth to some kind of new economics and that by riding the wave of technology, one can suddenly within a decade or half end up creating a quantum jump.

Alas! This is fiction. Desired, but improbable. I have no doubt that technology is enhancing speed of everything, including economics. In my book 'Transformers', I have demonstrated through logic how 'speed' is the next 'innovation'.

The US Dollars accumulated globally have to be reduced to sensible levels, these US Dollars have to be used to fuel American growth further with foreign investment, whereas the US has to produce more goods and services that will allow it to export more and repatriate US Dollars in return for the goods manufactured and exported.

The rate of investment reversal into US and its duration is a matter of mathematics and can be calculated easily. Such an investment reversal with possibility of competitive manufacturing in the US is now possible thanks to Industry 4.0 and automation of industrial processes, reducing labour costs to a minimum and making US products competitive on economies of scale.

All the aforementioned efforts to stabilize the sinking global economic system has to be accompanied with rationalization and entails the creation of an algorithmic exchange rate calculation ultimately, while meta-states could be established by the market towards setting a market driven exchange rate with algorithmic triggers and stoppers avoiding accidental run-overs. The ideally rational mechanism has been detailed in Chapter 4 of this book.

The question, I answered to myself in the affirmative was – "could we play a role in making the aforementioned (and necessary) macro-economic transformation happen"?

https://www.facebook.com/Indycia-108540784097382

To connect with us on email Scan QR below or mail@ connect@indycia.com

-------------------------------∞-----------------------------